Learning About Rocks

Sy Barlowe

D0043082

DOVER PUBLICATIONS, INC.
Mineola, New York

Introduction

You can find rocks just about everywhere! They come in a great variety of shapes, sizes, and colors. But all the different kinds of rocks fall into three main groups: igneous, sedimentary, and metamorphic. Igneous rocks are created by flowing lava from volcanoes. Sedimentary rocks are formed when fragments on the Earth's surface are moved and changed by water, wind, or ice. Metamorphic rocks are sedimentary or igneous rocks changed by heat, pressure, or chemical action. As you read, you will learn interesting facts about rocks and be able to illustrate each page with a colorful sticker. Perhaps you will decide to begin your own rock collection!

Granite

Granite is an igneous rock, formed when hot, flowing lava cools. Granite is an excellent building material because it is so strong. It may contain the minerals quartz, feldspar, or mica. Typical colors of granite are white, light gray, red, pink, and yellow, with bits of other colors as well. Some areas where granite is found are Canada, Russia, Africa, northwestern U.S., and northern Europe.

Obsidian

Obsidian is igneous rock that has cooled quickly. It usually has a glassy black texture but may be dark green to dark brown. Native Americans used obsidian for tools, arrowheads, and knives. This "volcanic glass" is found in areas where volcanic activity took place, such as the western U.S., Japan, and Italy. When polished, obsidian can be used to make jewelry.

Basalt

This igneous rock is the most common rock in the Earth's crust. It is formed when volcanic lava becomes solid. The layer beneath the ocean floor is basalt, formed when lava trapped below the Earth's surface cooled. Many of the rock specimens the Apollo astronauts brought back from the Moon were basalt. Basalt is found in India, Scotland, Iceland, Brazil, and parts of the U.S.

Diorite

The igneous rock diorite appears on the Earth's surface after the weathering away of certain other rocks. Its coloring is dark gray, blackish-gray, or a dull green. Today diorite is found chiefly in northern Europe, Scandinavia, Scotland, and parts of the U.S., such as Minnesota. It is used to construct buildings and roads.

1

2

3

4

5

6

AFTER ALL THE STICKERS HAVE BEEN PLACED IN THE CORRECT SPACES, PLEASE GENTLY REMOVE AND DISCARD THESE TWO PAGES.

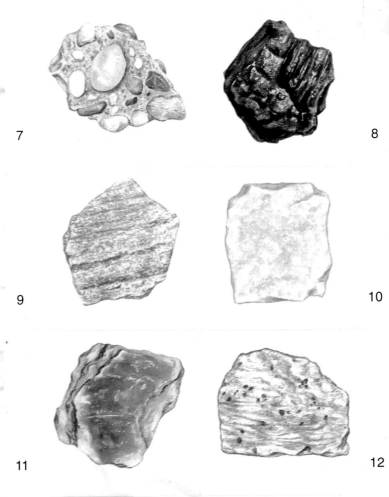

7

8

9

10

11

12

AFTER ALL THE STICKERS HAVE BEEN PLACED IN THE CORRECT SPACES, PLEASE GENTLY REMOVE AND DISCARD THESE TWO PAGES.   41291-1

Sandstone

Sandstone is a sedimentary rock made of grains of sand. These grains became cemented together over time. Sandstone may be white, light gray, yellowish, or dark red. Its size, color, and texture vary depending on where it came from. Many buildings in the eastern U.S. were constructed using this attractive rock. It is also found in central Europe.

Limestone

This sedimentary rock is found near water. It is usually made up of shells, corals, and the skeletons of early sea animals. The limestone pictured is millions of years old. Chalk is a soft form of limestone. Many buildings in the U.S. were built from Indiana limestone. Other areas containing limestone are the Appalachian and Rocky Mountain regions of the U.S., England, Germany, and Australia.

Conglomerates

Conglomerates are sedimentary rocks containing pebbles. They are formed when moving water such as that of a river cements together pebbles and sand. Because many materials form a conglomerate, the color varies greatly. This popular building stone is found in Great Britain and the eastern U.S. Conglomerates containing gold particles are found in South Africa.

Coal

A sedimentary rock, coal is formed from the remains of dead plants. Layers of this plant material build up over time, and pressure gradually turns the decaying matter into coal. This black or brownish black rock is produced and used in many parts of the world as fuel. Jet, one form of soft coal, is used to make jewelry after it has been polished.

Schist

Schist is metamorphic rock formed by great heat and pressure. It contains minerals such as mica and quartz. The eastern U.S., Scotland, the Alps, Japan, and New Zealand are several areas where it is found. Schist is sometimes used as gravel, but it also is used by artists and craftspersons. Ancient Egyptians made sculptures from schist, and today it is used to make pottery.

Slate

This metamorphic rock is actually shale that has been changed by pressure and heat over time. The minerals mica and quartz in shale have been pressed into layers. This means that slate can be split into smooth sheets, which helps in its use as roof tiles and chalkboards. The minerals in slate affect the rock's color, but slate is usually blue-gray, green, brown, or red.

Marble

Mountain limestone becomes marble when it is changed by heat and pressure over time. Pure marble is white. Other colors—yellow, green, brown, or black—reflect the minerals that have become part of the rock. Sculptors and builders prize this metamorphic rock, and it has been used to make many works of lasting beauty. It comes from Italy, Belgium, Ireland, Scotland, and parts of the U.S.

Gneiss

Gneiss (pronounced "nice") is a type of metamorphic rock formed very deep in the Earth's crust. It may contain bands of minerals such as mica or feldspar, which have been flattened into layers by heat and pressure over time. This rock, found in northern Europe and France, often is used as building stone. Its color varies depending on how it was formed.